THE THREE LITTLE PIGS TEACH GROWTH MINDSET

Hands-On Activities and Open-Ended Questions for Developing Grit, Adaptability and Creative Thinking in K–5 Classrooms

Will Hussey & Barry Hymer

Ulysses Press

Published in the US by:
ULYSSES PRESS
P.O. Box 3440
Berkeley, CA 94703
www.ulyssespress.com

First published in 2017 in Great Britain as *Puffed Out: The
Three Little Pigs' Guide to a Growth Mindset* by Crown House
Publishing Ltd.

ISBN 978-1-61243-902-0
Library of Congress Control Number: 2018967989

Printed in Canada by Marquis Book Printing
10 9 8 7 6 5 4 3 2 1

US proofreaders: Shayna Keyles, Renee Rutledge
Front cover and interior design: what!design @ whatweb.com
Cover art: pigs © Varlamova Lydmila/shutterstock.com;
    trees © Betelgejze/shutterstock.com
Interior art: © Les Evans

Distributed by Publishers Group West

CONTENTS

An Artful Note for the Teacher 5

Instructions: Know Matter 11

1. Pig or Small? 13

2. Law in Order? 15

3. Pork Wise? 18

4. Wolf Street-Cred...21

5. Trot Property...24

6. Hog Couture..27

7. Pig's Kin 31

8. The Four Trots...33

9. Ham Sandwich 36

10. Pig Tale...39

11. Pig Out 42

12. The Freeloading Little Pigs.................................45

13. Rash Decision..48

14. Pigs and Mortar 51

15. The Final Straw? 54

16. Crying Wolf..57

17. Neigh-borhood What? 60

18. Stick-Hay Fingers?..63

19. Teething Trouble 66

20. Foul Mouthed 69

21. Bacon Scroll 72

22. Pig Pocket?...75

23. Treading the Boars...78

24. Cheek by Jowl...81

25. Grime Scene Investigation (GSI)............................84

26. Howling Mad..87

27. Pig-Headed Start..90

28. Hair Do? 93

29. Dead End? 96

30. Feud and Think 99

31. Fit Fur Life? 102

32. 99SW9 105

33. Pot Luck? 108

34. Hungry for Love? 111

35. Make Believe 114

36. Pork Screw? 117

37. The Pursuit of Pork 120

38. Assault and Pepper 123

39. Faster Food 126

40. Cleaning Fluid? 129

41. Bred Maker 132

42. Huffing-Town Post 135

43. Pig E Day 138

44. A Pig Difference 141

45. Aeropig Capacity 144

46. Serendipiggy 147

47. Wood You Believe It? 150

48. Careless Whispork 153

49. Sty, Sty Again 156

50. Pork Jobs? 159

51. Un-men-tionable? 162

52. Cultural Cooperation 165

53. Basket Case 168

54. Boar-ed Stupid 171

55. Big Bad-Mouthing 174

56. Sow Far, Sow Good 177

57. Safe Sty? 180

58. Big Bad Language 183

59. Growth Mudset 186

60. Pulled Pork 189

Acknowledgments 192

AN ARTFUL NOTE
FOR THE TEACHER

Who knew the story of the three little pigs was so complicated, and so challenging? In fact, for decades adults have even been reading it to *infants*, as if it were a simple tale for simple kids! You've probably read it yourself or had it read to you in your crib. You might have read it to your students, or your own children. If you haven't, or you've forgotten it because it was so long ago, this is the essential plotline: Three pigs build a house each. A wolf exposes the limitations of two of the houses through lung power, but the third house remains standing. So he attempts to force an entry via the chimney and fails.

But this less-is-more version of the tale loses so much in its stripped-back state and would certainly not have been so popular for so many centuries in this form. In fact, it's more a case of less-is-even-less. Before you let your students loose on all the hidden challenges of the full and unedited story, here's a more worked-up version of the tale.

Three little pigs get thrown out by their mom to make their way in the world. It's not clear quite why she did this, or, if it ever were known, the reasons are lost in the mire (there are no mists of time). Perhaps she yearned for a quiet life after all those exhausting pig-rearing years. Perhaps she was being eaten out of barn and sty. Perhaps she wanted to bring her swine sweetheart 'round for a romantic candle-lit dinner and the little pigs would've ruined the atmosphere. Or perhaps (thinking the best of her), she knew the time had come for them to leave, and to keep them at home any longer would have been psychologically damaging, leaving them de-skilled and helplessly dependent. So possibly it was an act of selfless love. Anyway, whatever the reason, these were the days when it was still possible to get on the sty ladder, mortgages were freely available and the build-your-own-pigsty movement was just getting going. So it was a good time to waddle off into the wider world. And as far as we know, the pigs held no lasting grudges against their mom, so this doesn't turn into a dark slasher tale of deep hurt and eventual revenge.

The three turfed-out little pigs turned out to be quite resourceful little fellows after all, as conceivably predicted by their wise mom. (We say "fellows," but there's no hard evidence that they were male pigs at all, and we have a suspicion that at least two of them were female and victims of early sexism in the retelling—but that's our patriarchal society for you.) Although there's little reference to getting the landowner's permission, each little pig set about building his own house on a patch of greenbelt land. The youngest, apparently lazy and feckless in most retellings, but in reality probably just the least skilled by virtue of her youth, built a house made of straw. Nowadays she would be celebrated for her eco-credentials, but back then people thought straw houses were unstylish, flimsy and poorly insulated. Or maybe they knew even then that straw actually had outstanding insulation properties, but they just didn't care about climate change and the need to keep heating to a minimum to save the planet.

The middle brother went all Bear Grylls and built a perfectly adequate log cabin from a local wood store that just happened to have a "free wood—help yourself" sign beside it (and if you believe that you'll believe anything—actually, the middle pig was a light-fingered little good-for-nothing, but that's another story). Like straw, we know nowadays that wooden houses need not be rickety and ramshackle, and that wood is the building material of choice for many of the most warm, civilized and downright interesting nations in the world. Like Norway. But back then, anything other than solid stone, concrete or brick was considered passé. This is probably because the fledgling brick industry was gaining a stranglehold on the sty market and peddling their wicked lies, such as "Brick is best" and "If it ain't brick, we'll kick it down."

In the earliest known version of the tale (sponsored by Better Medieval Homes and Gardens), the eldest brother worked hard and purposefully, and some time after his younger sibs, finally completed his own home—built entirely of bricks, mortar, drywall plasterboard and dodgy 1970s gold-veined mirror tiles.

The rest of the tale involves the wolf, various taunting chants from the pigs (most of which seem to involve proud but rather tasteless boasting about their newly discovered facial hair), super-lupine blowing down of the first two houses, panicky fleeing of the first two pigs from house to house until they find sanctuary in their generous older brother's brick-built home, more hairy chinny-chin-chin taunting from the pigs, a desperate attempt by the wolf to enter the brick house Father Christmas–style, and, for the wolf, either a grisly demise in a fire roaring in the hearth or (for younger listeners) a hasty but non-life-changing retreat back up the chimney and a return to the woods, never to be seen or heard of again.

Now that you've been reminded of the story's basics, let's get down to the serious business of *really* understanding it. If your students can work their way through these 60 pig-related challenges without their brains hurting, we've probably not done justice to the story. And we certainly won't have helped their brains to grow. Because, as Professor Carol Dweck, originator of mindset theory tells us, a hurting brain is the feeling of a brain growing, so if they manage to persist, make mistakes and false starts, sweat them out and struggle to eventual success, then these little pigs will have helped you grow your students' brains. You will have changed their shapes and their structures and, what's more, they'll never be able to go back to their dull, lazy, fixed, pre-pig brains.

And that's our confession. This book might *seem* to be about the three little pigs, but to be honest, it's not really. The pigs are just the focus of our real purpose, which is to grow your students' brains by getting them to think between, above, below, around and beyond the lines. And once they've grown their brains by struggling through the challenges in this book, if you popped into a hospital equipped with the right machines and asked to see an MRI scan of their new pig-grown brains, you would be amazed at how many millions of new connections (synapses) you will have made between their brain nerves (neurons), and therefore how much more powerful their brains have become. And how much readier they now are to accept new challenges and to grow several million more neural connections.

And when you reach that point, you and your students might even be ready to tackle the fiendish complexities of "Goldilocks and the Three Bears" and the next stage of their endlessly growing and changing brains. But that's for another time. You'll need to get into training with those pigs first—good luck!

INSTRUCTIONS: KNOW MATTER

Thinking can be a funny business. Or alternatively, deadly serious. So maybe it would be more accurate to describe it as dead funny—in the case of this book, anyway. Immerse yourself within the pages and try to get to grips with an assortment of greased pigs. Be careful—they're slippery little buggers.

Take the chapter headings for starters; they might take some, err ... getting your head around. Those of you who think you could do better in this respect will notice that you're cordially invited to do so (a title should be earned, after all).

There's plenty to ponder, and if you require a nudge in the right direction, you will find three—although the direction you take depends on which way you're looking at it. Prompts and responses abound, although it's not always clear which is which; questions can be answered and answers should be questioned.

The Thinkantation encourages you to translate words into action—literally making sense and crafting meaning, putting the "ink" into "think." The editors' note is typically best ignored, and designed to derail your rationale—what do they know anyway? In addition to the ample food for thought, you'll also stumble across various asides, aboves and belows, intended to signpost the spectacular irrelevance.

Make of it what you will; prolonged exposure causes eye-watering, mind-altering growth something.

PIGGY PROMPTS

What does a Wolfie workout consist of?

What does a pig enjoy for a healthy snack?

How do you bribe a pig?

Some pigs have curlier tails than others; how do they feel about this?

1. PIG OR SMALL?

Your Title: ....

Ponder

The three pigs are described as "little." Are they too young to leave home? Should their parents be prosecuted for negligence?

Nudges

❧ Do you think the pigs are actually little? Compared to whom/what?

e.g., "No, I think they are an average size for a pig, but they seem very immature."

❧ Should the pigs have been allowed to leave home at such an early age?

e.g., "I think the pigs were too young to leave home and clearly weren't prepared for the outside world."

❧ Do you think the pigs were well cared for?

e.g., "Maybe the pigs were emotionally neglected by their parents, even though they were well fed."

Sticking points

Make sense of—"Prosecuted" means to legally accuse or hold someone accountable.

Understand—"Little" can refer to size or age.

Decipher—What constitutes "emotional negligence"? (Failing to look after someone's mind as well as their body.)

 ## Thinkantation

Create a life-size cut-out of one of the pigs.

 ## Editors' note

Sorry, some of these are pig questions, but well done for persevering. Does a pig actually enjoy a healthy snack?

2. LAW IN ORDER?

Your Title: ....

 Ponder

There is a notable absence of any law enforcement in the story. Why?

 Nudges

❥ Do you think the pigs were responsible for policing the town?

e.g., "Mr. Pig had just started his second tenure as sheriff, employing his sons as deputies. They were intent on cleaning up the town, before realizing they'd caused most of the mess."

❥ Why did the real police avoid the area?

e.g., "Porktown became a no-go area. Contract killing was rife."

❥ Undercover officers were rumored to have undertaken several covert missions. Were they successful?

e.g., "Yes, no one knows anything about them."

PIGGY PROMPTS

Criminal pigs have no honor; they will happily squeal on other gang members.

Police patrolling Porktown from the sky are affectionately known as "flying pigs."

Really—pigs can fly?

There is some disagreement over the number of thorns on the cactus.
It's a prickly subject.

Sticking points

M "Law enforcement" typically manifests as a
"force" appointed to police a community.

U Among criminals, "honor" is supposedly adhering
to a code where the police are not informed
under any circumstances.

D How might the police benefit from "criminal
collusion"? (Turning a blind eye enables all
parties to go about their business uninterrupted.)

 Thinkantation

Design and make a head to put a price on.

 Editors' note

There is no suggestion of collusion between
the police and the pigs; any truths are purely
coincidental.

3. PORK WISE?

Your Title: _____

Ponder

Why did the pigs not receive any helpful words of wisdom upon leaving home, and what should they have been told?

Nudges

- Were the pigs given any advice before they left home? If not, why not?

  e.g., "I think they were merely told that it was about time they found a place of their own."

- Do you think the pigs' parents had another motive for wanting them to leave home?

  e.g., "Mr. Pig wanted to convert two of the bedrooms into a billiard room."

- What advice would you have given to the pigs?

  e.g., "Don't always take the easiest option—and wear a disguise ..."

PIGGY PROMPTS

List the pigs' "blocked" websites.

Little Pig has some music stored on Sty Cloud. What are the most played tracks?

Do wolves prefer pork to lamb? Why?

Trotter? Instapig? What other social media apps can you think of?

Facepork is so yesterday.

The modern pig is social media savvy. Who might they follow on Trotter?

Sticking points

M A website is usually "blocked" because it might
contain inappropriate content.

U Being "social media savvy" suggests a
competence and familiarity with Twitter,
Facebook and other similar online forums.

D What is meant by "taking the easy option"?
(Pursuing a course of action with little likelihood
of encountering significant resistance.)

 Thinkantation

Make identity tags for the pigs to wear around their
necks in case of emergency.

 Editors' note

Can pigs use a touch screen? Maybe they would need
to use a stylus ...

4. WOLF STREET-CRED

Your Title: ....

Ponder

The wolf had already acquired a reputation for being both "big" and "bad." What happened prior to this particular escapade for him to acquire such notoriety?

Nudges

❥ What "bad" things has the wolf done?

e.g., "I think he went to get his claws polished but left the appointment without paying."

❥ In what ways is the wolf "big"?

e.g., "His head is big; he obviously thinks he's something special."

❥ Do you think the wolf enjoys his reputation?

e.g., "He seems to like all the attention, but really he is incredibly lonely."

PIGGY PROMPTS

Why does the wolf enjoy dressing
up in sheep's clothing?

Do sheep enjoy dressing up
in wolves' clothing?

Nose rings are so last season. What
is the latest pig accessory?

Some wolves have a preference for dressing
like sheep. Does this make them cross?

Sticking points

M "Acquiring a reputation" implies becoming known for behaving in a particular manner, often with negative connotations.

U "Cross dressing" describes the practice of wearing clothes that are typically associated with both genders (often at the same time).

D What does describing something as "last season" imply? Can you think of any examples?

 Thinkantation

Design a "wanted" poster for the wolf.

 Editors' note

Wolves undoubtedly suffer from negative stereotyping. (Can stereotyping be positive?)

5. TROT PROPERTY

Your Title: ....

Ponder

If the pigs are indeed "little," then why was more room required in the family home?

Nudges

- Why did the pigs no longer fit in the family home?

  e.g., "Middle Pig was expanding his business and needed room for the stock." Or "Little Pig was a hoarder; the place looked like a pigsty."

- Do you think there was a clash of personalities between some members of the family?

  e.g., "Big Pig held very different political views from those of his father (fascist pig!). Mr. Pig never lifted a trotter to help out around the house (sexist pig!)."

- How could the Pig family have better utilized their existing property to accommodate the whole family?

  e.g., "Build a pigger extension. Or simply invite the wolf to dinner."

PIGGY PROMPTS

Surely pigs retain the right to vote with their feet? Or at least with their trotters?

Name a famous French pig fashion designer.

Pigs often feign contempt. A snort can convey a wide spectrum of emotions. What else can a snort mean?

Really—pigs can vote?

Sticking points

M A "clash of personalities" describes when two people with contrasting behaviors and viewpoints antagonize each other.

U "Political views" typically encompass opinions regarding the best way to govern everyday dealings and practices in society. They can differ markedly from one person to another.

D What is meant by the term "voting with your feet"? (Undertaking action that directly relates to a strongly held viewpoint.)

 # Thinkantation

Design a campaign badge in support of one of the pigs' chosen political parties.

 # Editors' note

Pigs traditionally avoid thatched cottages. Moving house can often prove to be the last straw.

6. HOG COUTURE

Your Title: ....

Ponder

The pigs appear to be snappy dressers, a trait not normally associated with hogs. How have they acquired this penchant for haute couture?

Nudges

❥ Why do the pigs dress like they do? Are their outfits practical?

  e.g., "The pigs are hoping to go to art school, and like to express themselves."

❥ What is currently "hot to trot"?

  e.g., "Loose-fitting separates that mask ample tummies."

❥ How do the pigs recycle last season's clothing?

  e.g., "Donate them to charity. Many pigs seem to end up homeless."

PIGGY PROMPTS

Pigs are renowned for their modesty. You'll rarely catch one in just its underwear.

If pigs are snappy dressers, then what are crocodiles?

Do pigs struggle with laces? Are they ham-fisted?

Sticking points

M A "charity" is an organization that raises funds and awareness to promote and support a particular cause.

U "Camouflage" is the ability to disguise yourself among your surroundings.

D In what ways might someone "express" themselves? (Through their fashion, interests, pastimes, political viewpoints or language, for example.)

 Thinkantation

Design a logo for the Pig-Up fashion label.

 Editors' note

Combat pigs are experts in the art of deception and camouflage. You will never spot a pig hiding up a tree.

PIGGY PROMPTS

Blood is thicker than water (or friends are generally smarter than family).

Wolfie woz 'ere.

Sick as a pig: a good or bad thing? Discuss ...

7. PIG'S KIN

Your Title: ....

Ponder

How would you describe the relationship between the three siblings? The first two pigs ridiculed the third for his choice of building materials, but were nevertheless quick to seek help when faced with the wrath of the wolf.

Nudges

* Did all the pigs get along well? Perhaps two's company and three's a crowd?

   e.g., "I think that's just sibling rivalry."

* What did the first two pigs find so funny?

   e.g., "One of them had just attempted to explain how the world was created."

* How did Big Pig respond when his brother and sister came knocking at his door?

   e.g., "He welcomed them in (mistakenly thinking his pizza delivery had just arrived)."

Sticking points

M "Ridiculing" belittles a person, concept or idea that is found disagreeable.

U To "condone" a course of action means to overlook it despite knowing that it is wrong.

D What is the "Big Bang theory"? (The idea that the universe was created by an enormous explosion 13,600 million years ago.)

 # Thinkantation

Graffiti a poster with abusive terms that the siblings used to level at each other.

 # Editors' note

We do ~~not~~ condone vandalism.

8. THE FOUR TROTS

Your Title: ....

Ponder

Both the pigs and the wolf opted to move around on two legs instead of the conventional four—why?

Nudges

- How did the animals discover they could walk upright?

  e.g., "After a spending spree, the wolf found it easier to carry his shopping bags by walking on just two paws."

- Are there any activities that the animals can access on two legs that they couldn't manage on four?

  e.g., "Middle Pig has become more proficient at yoga."

- How do the traditionalist trotters view the more progressive uprights?

  e.g., "Dallying on two legs is disrespectful and bad for one's health; continued abuse may lead to blindness."

Sticking points

M A "society" is an organization or club formed for a particular purpose.

U "Freedom of expression" describes the right to hold an opinion and share it with others.

D Explain what is meant by a "traditionalist." (Someone who believes the old ways are still the best.)

 Thinkantation

Create a plaque for the POAF (Pigs-On-All-Fours) Society.

 Editors' note

POAF has recently been described as a "movement"—a movement rapidly gaining support.

PIGGY PROMPTS

What is the full name of the
Anti-POAF Society?

The Double-Up Society supports freedom of
expression and upright walking. Front-Up is
a splinter faction for the more agile porker.

According to the wolf, executing an
authentic wolf whistle requires the use
of two hands. Just where and how did
Wolfie procure the two hands required
for the aforementioned whistle?

9. HAM SANDWICH

Your Title: ....

Ponder

Did the pigs cohabit successfully prior to leaving the family home?

Nudges

❥ What were the pigs' sleeping arrangements?

e.g., "They shared a specially designed triple bunk bed."

❥ Did they share the household chores?

e.g., "Mr. Pig liked to delegate responsibilities, although not always evenly."

❥ Who spent the longest in the bathroom?

e.g., "Mrs. Pig followed an extensive beauty regimen, including carefully drawing a Gloucester Old Spot."

PIGGY PROMPTS

Pigs are not keen on awkward first dates; although, being pigs, they deal well with sticky moments.

Pigs don't like to behave impolitely, or do anything that might be construed as boar-ish.

Some deodorizers are described as a "breath of fresh air." Unsurprisingly, these are more popular with wolves than pigs.

Young pigs are renowned for being undisciplined. They're allowed to do what they want—hence, "pig-lets."

Sticking points

M "Cohabiting" means living under the same roof; sharing a home.

U "Delegating responsibility" refers to offloading chores and responsibilities on to others.

D What is meant by a "beauty regimen"? (The practices and procedures undertaken in order to maintain a certain appearance.)

 # Thinkantation

Design and make the packaging for a popular pig aftershave or perfume.

 # Editors' note

Personal hygiene is very important for a young pig. It's even more important for the older pigs who have to live with them.

10. PIG TALE

Your Title: ....

Ponder

Surely it's no coincidence that all three pigs left home simultaneously, seemingly unprepared for the challenges ahead. What's the *real* reason the three little pigs left home in such a hurry?

Nudges

- Mr. Pig is up to his neck in it. But what?

  e.g., "Stamp collecting: He can't seem to lick the habit."

- What drastic measures has Mrs. Pig resorted to in an effort to prevent the family home from being repossessed?

  e.g., "Scratching (and squealing) a living by various means."

- What is Mr. Pig afraid of? Whom does he owe money to?

  e.g., "A loan shark: Mr. Pig needs to save his bacon."

Sticking points

M Being "up to your neck in it" suggests being overwhelmed and overawed by one or a combination of factors.

U "Repossessed" usually refers to the act of having your home reclaimed, typically due to defaulting on loan repayments.

D How do you "scratch" a living? (Earning a living by whatever means possible.)

 ## Thinkantation

Design a set of special edition stamps to commemorate Mr. Pig's favorite movie.

 ## Editors' note

It's simply not true that all pigs like ballroom dancing. This is purely pink stereotyping.

PIGGY PROMPTS

Do any of the pig family have
a criminal record?

Pigs are not renowned for their taste
in music. Can you name a particularly
"criminal" record in their collection?

Have any of the pigs ever been in
a band? What was it called?

Pigs purportedly enjoy *Dancing with
the Swines*. What's the most popular
dance? Quickstep? Foxtrot? Wolfskip?

11. PIG OUT

Your Title: ....

Ponder

What effect did the departure of her three children have on Mrs. Pig?

Nudges

- Could it be that Mrs. Pig was having a secret affair and planned to reveal her adultery?

  e.g., "I think she was planning to move her lover, Hamlet, into the newly vacated bedroom."

- Perhaps Mrs. Pig was keen to extend her family further?

  e.g., "Mrs. Pig was desperate for another daughter, but until now there was no room for a nursery."

- Very little is known about Mrs. Pig. Could her role in the story be more significant than first thought?

  e.g., "Rumor has it that the wolf was spotted in a compromising clinch with Mrs. Pig, before leaving in a huff and a puff ..."

PIGGY PROMPTS

Typically, pigs can be described as "mo-hog-amous." How else could you describe them?

Mr. Pig remains apparently unaware of Mrs. Pig's alleged infidelity. He is either thick-skinned or just plain thick.

When quizzed on his involvement, Hamlet confessed to being "boared" and lonely. Can you think of a hobby that might keep him amused?

Rumors persist of a fourth pig. It is unclear what impact this might have on Middle Pig (or Joint Median Pig). Could you describe the other pigs mathematically?

Sticking points

M   In a "monogamous" relationship, an individual has only one partner.

U   "Infidelity" describes being unfaithful to a partner (and therefore not being monogamous).

D   What is a "compromising clinch"? (A warm embrace suggesting more than just friendship.)

 ## Thinkantation

Compose the love sonnet that Mrs. Pig received from her secret lover.

 ## Editors' note

Perhaps Wolfie was hungry for love. Or alternatively, just hungry.

12. THE FREELOADING LITTLE PIGS

Your Title: ....

Ponder

The pigs appear to have left home with very few possessions. When, where and how did they acquire the tools and equipment required for building their new houses?

Nudges

❧ Where did the pigs source the tools to build their homes?

e.g., "They went to school with a kangaroo named Joey who now runs a successful building and supply hardware store."

❧ Do you think the pigs needed guidance on using some of the machinery?

e.g., "Maybe—you can find all the instructions you need on the internet these days."

❧ Was there any part of the building process that the pigs chose not to undertake themselves?

e.g., "I believe they needed some help with the electrical wiring; this sort of intricate work can be tricky with trotters."

Sticking points

M "Freeloading" describes the actions of someone who benefits from the financial and material support of others, yet gives little in return.

U Tradesmen referred to as "cowboys" have dubious working practices that are likely to result in poor quality or unsafe construction or maintenance.

D What is meant by "calling in a favor"? (Requesting assistance in return for a previous act of goodwill.)

 Thinkantation

Devise an "early warning" intruder alarm for use in one of the pigs' houses.

 Editors' note

Pigs have acquired something of a reputation for being cowboy builders. Unsurprisingly, cows are taking legal action.[1]

---

1 Construct a better legal defense than merely asserting "it's all bull."

PIGGY PROMPTS

What is the name of Porktown's sister development?

What favor did the pigs call in with Joey the kangaroo?

Tricky with Trotters Expert Electrical Services is run by whom?

13. RASH DECISION

Your Title: ....

Ponder

The pigs settled on the location for their houses very quickly. What conclusions can you draw from this?

Nudges

➤ Had the pigs previously undertaken an extensive property search of the area?

   e.g., "Surveys of the area identified Porktown as a prosperous and sought-after location, popular with young upwardly mobile professional pigs (yuppigs)."

➤ Do you think pigs are impulsive by nature, making snap decisions?

   e.g., "They tend to rely on their considerable gut instinct."

➤ What makes Porktown so desirable?

   e.g., "Apparently there is a relatively low rate of recorded violent crime."

PIGGY PROMPTS

Who is the mayor of Porktown?

Who would like to be mayor of Porktown?

Pigs are not renowned for their financial acumen. If they were, they'd be known as "acupigs."

Sticking points

M "Financial acumen" describes the knowledge and insight required to invest money wisely.

U A "property search" describes the process of searching for potential homes worthy of further consideration.

D What constitutes a "desirable" place to live? (Typically, somewhere that is safe, well-resourced, picturesque and relatively free from anti-social behavior.)

 ## Thinkantation

Design and make a new set of counters for a "Three Little Pigs" themed real-estate board game.

 ## Editors' note

Recorded violent crime is typically low in Porktown; the pigs seldom get the chance to record it.

14. PIGS AND MORTAR

Your Title: ....

Ponder

Why did the pigs opt to build the properties themselves? Most prospective homeowners opt to buy or rent new accommodations, leaving the construction work to the experts.

Nudges

⟩ What credentials did the pigs possess for construction work?

e.g., "Not many. I think they'd built a few sandcastles on the beach last summer."

⟩ Do you think the pigs saved money by undertaking the work themselves?

e.g., "No, because two of the pigs would eventually have to rebuild their houses."

⟩ Would the pigs have been able to secure a mortgage enabling them to buy a home? Home loins can be hard to come by ...

e.g., "I don't think they would have been able to save the necessary down payment."

PIGGY PROMPTS

Why did all the pigs build bungalows? Perhaps they should have set their aspirations higher.

"Pigs are responsible for putting the sty into style," according to which popular animal home-décor magazine?

How did the wolf develop such an impressive VO_2 capacity? Did he work out or simply pig-out?

The wolf was obviously full of hot air. What did he brag about?

Sticking points

M Buying a property typically involves borrowing money to purchase the house (a mortgage), which is usually paid back over the course of some years. Renting describes paying the owner (landlord) for the privilege of using their property.

U A "down payment" is usually required when securing a mortgage. This is a sum of money to be paid by the prospective homeowner on agreement of the loan.

D What is a "VO_2 capacity"? (The maximum rate of oxygen the body can consume during exercise. It is usually a good indicator of physical fitness.)

 # Thinkantation

Construct a scale model of one of the pigs' houses (pre-demolition).

 # Editors' note

Pigs are notorious for starting things they cannot ...

15. THE FINAL STRAW?

Your Title: ....

Ponder

Little Pig was the first to complete her new build.
This suggests an accomplished craftspig, working
skillfully with specialized materials. How come?

Nudges

🢂 Where did Little Pig learn to weave straw?

    e.g., "Her great grandfather thatched the family
home some years ago."

🢂 Does the speed of the build suggest Little Pig was
a master in her field?

    e.g., "No, the field actually belonged to Farmer
Abraham."[2]

🢂 Was there a catastrophic flaw in the design?

    e.g., "Not only the floor, but the walls and roof
were not sufficiently load bearing."

---

2   Not to be confused with his ecclesiastical cousin, Father
Abraham, who had seven sons.

PIGGY PROMPTS

How did great grandfather meet his maker?

What was the name of the three little pigs' great grandfather (now sadly deceased)?

Who was great grandfather's maker, anyway?

Sticking points

M A "thatcher" is proficient at covering roofs with materials such as straw or rushes, layering them in such a way that water is diverted from the supporting structure.

U A "catastrophic flaw" describes a serious weakness that inevitably leads to the destruction or failure of a building, system or process.

D What is meant by a "cottage" industry? (A small-scale operation undertaken at home, usually by family members.)

 Thinkantation

Design and build a residence that will collapse in just one puff.

 Editors' note

Pigs have a rich history of cottage industry. Wolves, by contrast, lean toward future technologies: specifically blew-chip industries.

16. CRYING WOLF

Your Title: ....

Ponder

The wolf verbally warned each of the pigs upon arrival that he would blow their house down. Why did he forego the element of surprise?

Nudges

- What's with all the commotion?

  e.g., "Wolves, by nature, are full of hot air. They're keen to maximize their exposure."

- But why does the wolf have to be so loud? Surely this presents the pigs with an opportunity to give him the slip?

  e.g., "Some historians suggest that pigs are actually petrified of loud noises. Indeed, there is evidence to suggest that current practice has evolved from 'huffing and puffing' to 'bellowing' the house down."

- Does the wolf show some compassion by announcing his arrival, thus providing the pigs with an opportunity to escape?

  e.g., "Wolves still maintain the upper paw in a pig hunt."

Sticking points

M "The element of surprise" describes the perceived benefit gained from embarking upon an unexpected course of action unannounced.

U "Compassion" means having pity and concern for the sufferings of others.

D What does "putting on a front" mean? (Pretending to feel a certain way.)

 Thinkantation

Design and make a saber for the wolf to rattle.

 Editors' note

Cows are very sensitive to accusations of cowardice. The Union of Bovines (UoB) positions itself as the nation's agricultural backbone.

PIGGY PROMPTS

What is the name of the wolf's
PR company?

What is the most cowardly creature?

Wolves don't like to be accused of
crying and tend to put on a front.

Perhaps the wolf has a pig fixation.
Or a fig pixilation.

17. NEIGH-BORHOOD WHAT?

Your Title: ....

 Ponder

Who else might have lived in the pigs' neighborhood? Why did the wolf not pay them a visit?

 Nudges

❧ Who lived on the opposite side of the street, at numbers 4 and 6 Porktown?

e.g., "An estranged couple of horses. They were never a stable family."

❧ Why was the wolf so fixated on the three little pigs?

e.g., "These pigs looked particularly appetizing. They were the pig of the bunch."

❧ How did the other residents go unnoticed?

e.g., "They had received military survival training for just such an eventuality, learning how to blend in to their surroundings."[3]

---

3 The training course is entitled "Gray Is the New Pink," should you be interested.

PIGGY PROMPTS

If the wolf has a secret collection of pixilated fig photos, does he harbor any other peculiar interests?

The survival training course is delivered by the Old Navy, trained killers who know how to find an affordable yet chic outfit.

Sticking points

M The term "special forces" usually refers to elite military units.

U "Estranged" refers to people who are no longer on friendly terms with each other.

D What is meant by becoming "fixated"? (Forming an obsessive attachment to someone or something.)

 ## Thinkantation

Create a photographic portfolio, camouflaging a pig in every shot.

 ## Editors' note

Killer heels can be lethal in the wrong hands. Or on the right trotters.

18. STICK-HAY FINGERS?

Your Title: ....

Ponder

What was the reasoning behind the pigs' choice of specialized building materials?

Nudges

- What was the attraction of the sticks and the hay? They're hardly substantial.

  e.g., "The best things in life are free, and besides, it worked for the ancient Greeks."

- Did the first two pigs make a conscious decision to go with sticks and hay?

  e.g., "No, they used whatever they stumbled upon first. If they'd walked in a different direction they might have used donated clothing."

- Do you think that bricks are overrated?

  e.g., "They're okay if you want to stay put in one place, but sticks and hay allow you to go where the wind blows."

Sticking points

M A "specialized building material" is a medium that requires additional knowledge or expertise to manipulate.

U "Overrated" refers to someone or something that is considered better or more important than it actually is.

D What is meant by the phrase "the best things in life are free"? (Simple pleasures, such as enjoying a walk on a summer's day, are often far more enjoyable and easily accessible than material gains.)

 ## Thinkantation

Draw some of the items found in the Porktown donation bags out for pick-up.

 ## Editors' note

Fundraising is supposed to be fun. Unless it's not your (charity) bag.

PIGGY PROMPTS

What's up with the title? Pigs don't even have fingers!

Do pigs make good thieves?

If fundraising raises funds, does hair-raising raise hay?

19. TEETHING TROUBLE

Your Title: ....

Ponder

Do you think the wolf's actions are truly representative of the wolf species, or merely the misguided actions of one slightly unhinged individual?

Nudges

❥ Have you ever heard anyone say a good word about a wolf?

e.g., "Apparently wolves are well respected in some animal communities. Unsurprisingly, you won't hear a good word about them; animals don't tend to talk."

❥ Wolves seem to receive bad press. Can you think of a positive wolf role model?

e.g., "A good wolf is admittedly hard to find. They're even harder to shake off once you've found one." #LittleRedRidingHood

❥ Maybe the wolf is a force for good. Can you put a positive spin on Wolfie?

e.g., "Perhaps the wolf's actions are justified: He was merely keeping the unruly pig community in check by providing a strong deterrent."

PIGGY PROMPTS

What else is currently trending on Trotter? #LRRH

Who are the candidates standing in opposition to the wolf?

"Greedy little oinks." How else can you smear the pigs?

Hungry. Can you think of another good word for the wolf?

Sticking points

M A "political advertisement" is a television or radio broadcast made by a political party, encouraging voters to support their election.

U "Bad press" describes negative criticism that is reported by one or more sources.

D Can you explain what is meant by "positive spin"? (To make a situation sound better than it actually is.)

 ## Thinkantation

Record a short political advertisement, campaigning to elect Wolfie as the mayor of Porktown.

 ## Editors' note

Wolves make good mayors (or night-mayors, if you're a pig).

20. FOUL MOUTHED

Your Title: ....

Ponder

In reality, the wolf must have deployed more than mere halitosis to demolish the pigs' houses. How did he manage it?

Nudges

- It is rumored that the wolf had high-tech gadgetry: What did he have in his arsenal?

    e.g., "The Air-in-the-Community (AC3000) is purpose built to curtail urban sprawl."

- Some say Wolfie had been taking performance-enhancing steroids. Does this explain his super-human abilities?

    e.g., "The wolf would do anything he could to get yoked, even trespass on farmyard properties."

- Rumors persist that there was actually more than one wolf. Can you confirm or deny this?

    e.g., "Forensic analysis of the scene suggested simultaneous puffing from multiple angles. The wolf had company."

Sticking points

M "Halitosis" is more commonly known as bad (or smelly) breath.

U "Steroids" are drugs that are sometimes used to illegally boost physical performance.

D Can you explain what is meant by "forensic analysis"? (It refers to the use of science to gather, examine and analyze potential evidence.)

 Thinkantation

Design and create a replica of the AC3000.

 Editors' note

Wolves have psychopathic tendencies; fanger-management issues are common.

PIGGY PROMPTS

How else does a pig defend itself?

Modern day pigs are encouraged to take self-defense classes. The "pork chop" can be a highly effective tactic.

The Pigs Liberation Front (PLF) is committed to reclaiming all land forcibly occupied by wolves. Lawyers for the wolves say they will not engage in any public mud-slinging.

21. BACON SCROLL

Your Title: ....

Ponder

Newly declassified government papers suggest a long-running vendetta between the pig and wolf families. How did the feud come about?

Nudges

❥ The wolf and pigs reputedly had shared interests. What business were they involved in?

   e.g., "Illegal cake trafficking: smuggling banned ingredients through the forest by means of red-hooded couriers."

❥ How did the partnership end?

   e.g., "The wood-cutter acted on an anonymous tip-off, rumored to be from a pig."

❥ Why did the pigs want to end the business partnership?

   e.g., "Pigs are greedy. They wanted to maximize their share of the profits."

PIGGY PROMPTS

"Greedy pigs" are referred to as such because they don't just want to take their cake and eat it; they want to make a small fortune in the process.

After having the "whistle blown" on their illegal activities, the term "wolf whistle" filtered into common parlance.

"Wolf whistling" is commonly regarded as rude or offensive. Which is probably why the wolf does it.

After the wolves were prosecuted for their involvement in cake trafficking, how did the pigs diversify their business interests?

Sticking points

M "Declassified" papers are no longer top secret.

U A "shared interest" typically refers to a transaction or concern that can affect more than one person.

D Describe what is meant by "trafficking." (Illegally moving people or goods for profit or gain.)

 ## Thinkantation

Make a cake for smuggling in a wicker basket.

 ## Editors' note

Cakes were legally prohibited due to escalating attacks on grandmas.

22. PIG POCKET?

Your Title: ....

Ponder

It is doubtful that a wolf can make a living solely from hounding (little) pigs. Does the wolf have a sideline?

Nudges

❥ Pork is readily available in stores. Where does the wolf fit in?

e.g., "Usually the farmer deals directly with food outlets. For less compliant pigs, the services of a bounty hunter may be required."

❥ Where do a wolf's strengths lie?

e.g., "A wolf trades off his teeth. Many wolves offer protection—sometimes even when it hasn't been requested."

❥ Are they comfortable with digital marketing?

e.g., "Wolves are becoming increasingly online savvy. Virtual 'huffing' apps are currently under development."

PIGGY PROMPTS

What causes a wolf to become vegetarian?

Wolves have lobbied the government
for the right to make a decent living.
They've got to eat, after all ...

Wolves are sometimes painted as
caring animals. Probably because
no authentic photographs exist.

Can a wolf be employed by a pig? Is it too
tempting to bite the hand that feeds you?

Sticking points

M "Making a living" is a euphemism for describing someone's occupation.

U "Bounty hunters" can be hired to carry out questionable tasks—at a price.

D What is "digital marketing"? (The strategies used to advertise products or services online.)

 Thinkantation

Advertise the wolf's range of services. Be sure to showcase the full extent of his portfolio.

 Editors' note

Wolves are investing heavily in pay-day loan companies. Loan sharks are increasingly making way for lone wolves.

23. TREADING THE BOARS

Your Title: ....

Ponder

The whole unfortunate episode was a bit of a performance. Do the pigs have a theatrical background?

Nudges

- All three pigs display some nifty footwork. Have they had any formal training?

  e.g., "No, but Middle Pig once co-starred with a wolf in a Porky Players' production of *Gone with the Wind*."

- Do any of the pigs have a specific talent?

  e.g., "Mrs. Pig does a neat party trick with a roast apple."

- Would you say any of the pigs have become typecast?

  e.g., "Big Pig often plays a dirty 'trotten' scoundrel."

PIGGY PROMPTS

Acquire the autographs of the leading cast members.

The original cast of "The Three Little Pigs" was sacked. What for?

The wolf's signature act is affectionately referred to as "the hog roast." But not by the pigs.

Who is conducting the orchestra?

Sticking points

M An "unfortunate episode" typically describes an event with undesirable consequences.

U Some dancers and musicians receive "formal training," such as ballet or tap-dancing classes.

D What is meant by becoming "typecast"? (Being associated with a particular type of character or role, to the extent that it would be difficult to take on a contrasting part.)

 Thinkantation

List the song titles included in *The Three Little Pigs—The Musical*.

 Editors' note

"The Three Substantial Heifers" probably wouldn't have achieved the same critical acclaim.

24. CHEEK BY JOWL

Your Title: ....

Ponder

The pigs decided to build their homes practically next door to each other, so why didn't they combine their resources to develop one large, luxury living space?

Nudges

🐖 Are pigs capable of making decisions independently, or are they adversely affected by socioeconomic factors?

e.g., "Pigs are strong willed and stubborn (and they have no idea what 'socioeconomic factors' are)."

🐖 Do pigs possess a strong family bond that can stifle individual character development?

e.g., "Greed is the overriding factor. In shared accommodations, a pig has the possibility of an additional two portions of breakfast (if he's quick)."

🐖 Are three front doors better than one?

e.g., "Yes. It takes the wolf three times as long to break down three doors than one."

PIGGY PROMPTS

What makes pigs stick together
(apart from mud)?

If the pigs shared an apartment, they
wouldn't be apart. Maybe "togetherment"
would have been more appropriate?

No one likes junk mail.
Doors should be fitted with the more
discerning "don't letter" box.

Can you think of an alternative
name for house number 3?
"Draft Excluder" perhaps?

Sticking points

M "Socioeconomic factors" describe how the amount of money you have or where you go to school can influence your role in society.

U An "overriding factor" tends to be the most important consideration.

D What is meant by the term "a strong family bond"? (Siblings feel compelled to look after each other.)

 Thinkantation

Compose a melody for one of the pigs' doorbells. Lyrics are optional.

 Editors' note

The concept of a front door is relatively new to a pig. For years they have been content with merely an opening. Hence you will never hear a pig knock (but will likely see one run).

25. GRIME SCENE INVESTIGATION (GSI)

Your Title: ....

Ponder

The remains of the first two pigs' houses were reportedly scattered over a wide area. Did the wolf find anything of interest?

Nudges

❯ Was anything of value recovered?

e.g., "A supposedly 'lost' piece of artwork by the well-known cubist sculptor and artist Pigasso was uncovered."

❯ Do you think the pigs were materialistic?

e.g., "The pigs are representative of today's modern consumerist culture—literally consuming just about anything and everything."

❯ Was there any evidence linking the wolf directly to the crime?

e.g., "Interestingly, the scene was devoid of any conclusive forensic evidence. Probably because it was also devoid of any forensic scientists."

PIGGY PROMPTS

Young wolves are very interested
in cubism—or wolf cub-ism.

Name three of DJ Pork's top 10 hits.

Sticking points

M "Cubism" refers to a style of artwork that typically makes use of geometrical shapes and lines.

U Gathering "forensic evidence" usually requires an element of scientific and technological investigation.

D What is meant by a "consumerist culture"? (The population are keen to acquire ever-increasing amounts of goods and services.)

 ## Thinkantation

Replicate the "lost" Pigasso.

 ## Editors' note

DJ Pork once arrived to spin the decks at the wolf's house, only to find he'd been invited to a hog roast. Wolves and pigs have very different perceptions of a turntable.

26. HOWLING MAD

Your Title: ....

Ponder

The wolf's behavior can be a little unpredictable.
Do you think he would benefit from mindfulness
training?

Nudges

➤ Is all that huffing and puffing really the best
   strategy?

   e.g., "Yes. Why change a winning formula?"

➤ Perhaps the wolf is devoid of alternative ideas?

   e.g., "Wolves typically play the long game,
   believing that any obstacles will blow over soon."

➤ Wolfie was seen collecting a prescription earlier
   that day. Was he on something?

   e.g., "A course of 'bad medicine' to boost his
   villainous credentials."

Sticking points

M An "affliction" is another way of describing something that causes great pain or suffering.

U A "winning formula" is a strategy that has been successful when used in the past.

D What is meant by playing the "long game"? (Remaining focused on a goal that might take some time to achieve.)

 Thinkantation

Create the label for Wolfie's prescription medication.

 Editors' note

The wolf had clearly not been taking his antacids—for the relief of bloating and the pain of trapped wind.

PIGGY PROMPTS

Describe the wolf's afflictions
that require medicating.

If a wolf can be described as a little
unstable, how would you best describe
a slightly deranged horse?

Should the wolf see a doctor or a vet?

There's strong evidence to suggest
that the wolf required greater care in
the community. Who was responsible
for his (lack of) supervision?

27. PIG-HEADED START

Your Title: ....

Ponder

The wolf sets off in hot pursuit of the first two pigs, but to little avail. Why doesn't he catch up?

Nudges

▶ Do you think the pigs are particularly fast, or that Wolfie just hasn't got what it takes?

  e.g., "The pigs run like greased lightning, and the wolf is probably a little out of puff."

▶ Does the wolf deliberately allow the first two pigs to escape his clutches?

  e.g., "Wolfie knows that it wouldn't be much of a story if everything was over in the first breath."

▶ Is the wolf particularly nasty—trying to prolong the pigs' agony?

  e.g., "Wolfie just wanted to give them pause for thought. In fact, four paws for thought."

PIGGY PROMPTS

Pigs are known to suffer from a weak bladder. They worry someone's going to use it for a soccer game.

Is the wolf a victim of entrapment?

Some say Wolfie inspired the concept of fast food. What does a McWolfie Happy Meal consist of?

Sticking points

M "Entrapment" describes the act of tempting someone to commit a crime that they would be otherwise unlikely to commit.

U Early soccer balls were made from an inflated pig's bladder.

D How would you describe the concept of "fast food"? (Mass-produced food that is prepared and served relatively quickly.)

 Thinkantation

Create a timing device to measure how fast the pigs can run.

 Editors' note

While wolves often get bad press, it has to be said that pigs can be des-pig-able.

28. HAIR DO?

Your Title: ....

Ponder

The pigs exclaim that they won't let the wolf in, "not by the hair of their chinny chin chin." What's the significance?

Nudges

> Do pigs suffer from premature balding?

e.g., "Facial hair is a sign of virility for male pigs. Celebrity icons typically sport waxed mustaches and jaunty mutton chops."

> Would a pig rather do anything than shave the hair off his chin?

e.g., "Absolutely, a pig would rather a close shave than an actual shave any day."

> Does the wolf have a reputation for shaving his victims?

e.g., "Wolfie is also known as 'The Smooth Criminal.'"

Sticking points

M "Premature balding" describes the process of losing your hair at a relatively young age.

U The "highest grossing" films are the ones that make the most money through sales at the box office.

D How would you describe someone's "formative years"? (The first few years of a child's life, when a great deal of learning and physical development occurs.)

 # Thinkantation

Construct a false beard for a pig who requires additional facial hair.

 # Editors' note

Did you know that hair transplants were the most common cosmetic procedures undertaken by pigs last year? Fur real.

PIGGY PROMPTS

Wolfie's profile appears rather unstable. Can you describe his troubled formative years?

Jean-Claude Van Hamme has millions of Trotter followers.

List the top ten highest grossing animal film stars.

Blush is popular with pigs of both sexes. If only the three little pigs had applied a little more concealer.

29. DEAD END?

Your Title: ....

Ponder

There are conflicting reports about how the story ends. Did the wolf live to fight another day?

Nudges

- The wolf suffered third degree burns in the cooking pot. Could he really survive such serious injuries?

  e.g., "Fortunately (for the wolf) medical assistance was close at hand."

- Do you think wolves are born survivors?

  e.g., "No, but they are dead stubborn."

- Do you think the wolf didn't actually survive, and his ghost returned to haunt the residents of Porktown?

  e.g., "Pigs don't believe in such mumbo-jumbo. Unless it's a full moon, of course ..."

PIGGY PROMPTS

A paramedic happened to be passing. Whom had she just finished attending to?

The Latin for wolf is *Canis lupus*. The *Canisn't lupus* is long extinct.

Why don't pigs cook with an oven like the rest of us?

Apparently wolf meat is rather tough if not boiled. Hence, young pigs are taught from an early age not to dry wolf.

Sticking points

M "Conflicting reports" describe the same event in very different ways.

U A "third degree" burn is a serious skin injury that can take a long time to heal.

D What is meant by the term "born survivor"? (Someone who consistently displays the resilience and ability to overcome adversity.)

 Thinkantation

Construct a tripod out of natural materials to support a cooking pot. Ask permission before you add the wolf.

 Editors' note

Goldilocks has received a police warning for making inappropriate calls to emergency services. An official spokesperson called it "bear-faced cheek."

30. FEUD AND THINK

Your Title: ....

Ponder

Potted wolf is something of a pig delicacy. Does this cause significant inter-species tension?

Nudges

- Is there some sort of legislation to discourage cooking your neighbor?

  e.g., "No, a legal loophole doesn't discriminate between cooking for your neighbor and cooking your actual neighbor."

- Is there a more efficient way of cooking wolf than using a large pot?

  e.g., "Microwaves are arguably quicker and easier—that is, if you can manage to close the door."

- How is wolf best served?

  e.g., "With lightly sautéed potatoes and a side salad. The wolf has personally expressed a preference for being served rare (in fact, non-existent)."

PIGGY PROMPTS

What is the name of the well-known Michelin-starred pig eatery?

Wolves are not to be eaten on religious grounds. Outside the church gates is fine, however.

Wolf is best served blue. Or blew.

Wait is a sensitive topic for pigs. They like courses to follow in quick succession.

Sticking points

M A "delicacy" usually refers to a rare or expensive food item that is considered highly desirable.

U "Michelin stars" are awarded to restaurants in recognition of fine dining.

D What makes a menu "à la carte"? (A wide variety of choice is available in many combinations, rather than "set" meals.)

 Thinkantation

Create a three-course à la carte menu for a celebrated pig eatery.

 Editors' note

Wolves like pig curry. Hungry wolves like hurried pork.

31. FIT FUR LIFE?

Your Title: ....

Ponder

The sport and leisure industry is a growth sector for pigs and wolves alike. Why?

Nudges

- Why is there such an increase in gym membership?

  e.g., "Animals have become more body aware."

- Is keeping fit necessary for survival in today's dog-eat-dog society?

  e.g., "Pigs need to be able to sprint. Wolves need to be able to swim."

- Is there evidence to suggest that animals are adopting a more holistic approach to health and well-being?

  e.g., "No, many wolves still suffer from anxiety (particularly the fear of being submerged in a cooking pot)."

PIGGY PROMPTS

Visits by pigs to health spas are up by 50%. Mudpacks are the most popular treatment.

Name a popular brand of animal sportswear.

Bears often make the best yogis.

Which new sport is to be included in the next Animal Olympics?

Sticking points

M To be "body aware" suggests an appreciation of
health and physical appearance.

U A "holistic approach" often refers to treating
general health and well-being rather than specific
complaints.

D What are the symptoms of "anxiety"? (These can
vary widely but may include feelings of panic,
fear and nausea.)

 Thinkantation

Design a yoga pamphlet with positions for the
beginner-to-intermediate pig.

 Editors' note

Pigs are among the healthiest members of society.
Figures suggest they are generally eaten before
being struck down by any of the recognized "big
killers."

32. 99SW9

Your Title: ....

Ponder

Porktown seems devoid of any of the conventional emergency services. How did the residents manage?

Nudges

❧ Were there any established procedures in the event of a fire?

e.g., "While the pigs would make haste, any wolves in the vicinity were quick to arrive armed with BBQ sauce."

❧ What happened if an animal was taken seriously ill?

e.g., "Most animals were never taken seriously, even if they were ill."

❧ Which illnesses were most common in Porktown?

e.g., "Wolves are renowned for suffering cardiac arrest; excessive huffing and puffing puts considerable strain on the heart and lungs."

Sticking points

M The "conventional emergency services" comprise the fire department, police and ambulance response.

U British police patrol vehicles are sometimes referred to as "panda cars," referencing the original two-tone colors of early police cars.

D Describe the purpose of a "defibrillator." (A device used to deliver a therapeutic dose of electricity to the heart, in order to re-establish a normal heartbeat.)

 # Thinkantation

Mock up a wolf defibrillator. Remember to stand well clear when you've finished.

 # Editors' note

Pigs have a distinct recovery position: a minimum distance of one mile from the nearest wolf.

PIGGY PROMPTS

A wolf would probably object to riding in a panda car. How would you rebrand it?

What derogatory term would you devise for a member of the hog constabulary?

Accidents are relatively rare. Gratuitous violence, however, is common.

Would it be insensitive to expect a pig to travel in a panda car?

What sort of a car would a panda ride in?

33. POT LUCK?

Your Title: ....

Ponder

Why did Wolfie choose the chimney to make his move?

Nudges

❥ Do you think the wolf gave sufficient consideration to his plan of attack?

 e.g., "Wolfie was prepared for an aerial assault, but Little Pig was waiting with the table salt."

❥ Where did the wolf learn to rappel?

 e.g., "Climbing and mountain craft have long been essential for the aspiring sheep rustler. Many animals are found grazing in inaccessible places while being guarded by absent-minded boys."

❥ Surely the chimney always looked a risky entry point?

 e.g., "Intelligence recommended it as a genuinely viable option. Chimneys are purportedly accessed every Christmas."

PIGGY PROMPTS

Why didn't the wolf use the skylight instead?

Certain sheep have acquired a taste for extreme sports. Certain wolves have acquired a taste for sheep.

Who was piloting the helicopter?

Wolves obviously like to make an entrance. What does this say about the species? (As opposed to ducks, for example, who are keen to make a splash.)

Sticking points

M "Rappelling" describes the process of controlled descent from an elevated position by means of a rope and a safety mechanism (belay).

U Gathering "intelligence" describes the process of acquiring information relating to an identified threat or foe. Sometimes the term refers to the organization collecting and analyzing the data.

D What makes a model "to scale"? (A proportional representation of a particular object, usually smaller than the original.)

 Thinkantation

Craft a scale model of the wolf and Little Pig to compare their sizes.

 Editors' note

Wolves' (lack of) spatial awareness can be their downfall. (The most notable example is the notorious "My, what a big [insert grossly disproportionate physical feature] you have, Grandma" scenario.)

34. HUNGRY FOR LOVE?

Your Title: ....

Ponder

Apparently, behind every successful man is a woman. Could the wolf have been influenced by a love interest?

Nudges

❥ What drove the wolf to act so irrationally?

> e.g., "A desire to prove himself as a worthy suitor and bring home the bacon."

❥ How did Wolfie meet his mystery lady?

> e.g., "He joined a niche dating agency: *The Huffington Most* aims to match wolves who have a fondness for hot air."

❥ Do you think the wolf's girlfriend should have kept him on the straight and narrow?

> e.g., "No, her morals were questionable to say the least. She was a big bad influence."

Sticking points

M To behave "irrationally" means to think, talk or act without giving due consideration or reason to a situation.

U "Niche" refers to a position or organization that is particularly suited to someone's talents or personality.

D What is meant by "questionable morals"? (Behaving in accordance with beliefs that deviate from widely accepted views of honesty and fair play.)

 ## Thinkantation

Draft Wolfie's online profile for *The Huffington Most* (150 words maximum).

 ## Editors' note

The pair had a volatile relationship; she batted her eyelids and he battered down doors.

PIGGY PROMPTS

Who did Wolfie hook up with on
previous dates?

If music is the food of love,
then what is pork?

Name a popular wolf love potion.

What is the name of Wolfie's girlfriend?

35. MAKE BELIEVE

Your Title: ....

Ponder

Some describe the pigs' escape as nothing short of miraculous. Did the three little pigs benefit from divine intervention?

Nudges

- Were any of the pigs religious?

  e.g., "The family were all believers in Hog, but were not active members of the church community."

- How do you explain their lucky escape from the jaws of the wolf?

  e.g., "What goes around comes around. The wolf landed himself in hot water."

- Did the pigs' narrow escape give their lives renewed purpose?

  e.g., "Middle Pig went on to form the Piggy's Trust, a conciliatory organization committed to building bridges within the community."

PIGGY PROMPTS

Does a pig wear a dog collar?
Does a dog wear a pig collar?

Tellingly, no wolves have yet affiliated
to the Piggy's Trust.

Name the other four members
of the Piggy's Trust.

The Repentant Wolves Society (also
known as "Suck It Up") have struggled
for new members. Or old members.

Sticking points

M "Divine intervention" suggests that a miraculous event has taken place, the magnitude or unlikelihood of which suggests the involvement of (a) God.

U A "narrow escape" suggests that someone has survived a hazardous encounter—but only just.

D What is meant by a "conciliatory organization"? (A group committed to helping to resolve disputes between individuals and parties in disagreement.)

 ## Thinkantation

Create and photograph a shrine dedicated to the Hog Almighty.

 ## Editors' note

Many pigs are "apigist": living their lives without subscribing to the teachings of the Hog Almighty.

36. PORK SCREW?

Your Title: ....

Ponder

Conspiracy theories abound: Was there more to this story than meets the eye?

Nudges

❥ There are rumors of a mysterious fourth pig seen lurking behind a grassy knoll. Who could this have been?

  e.g., "Whoever it was purportedly bore a family resemblance—a 'wronged' cousin perhaps?"

❥ Prior to the incident, wolves had received a boost in public opinion polls—a boost that was subsequently short lived. Were there hidden forces at work?

  e.g., "Councillor Fang Django was touted as a potential leader of Porktown's Town Council. Support later subsided, with Django complaining of a smear campaign."

❥ Photographic footage has been examined by experts, with several suggesting the shadows are in the wrong place. How come?

  e.g., "There is a theory among certain members of the wolf community that the "huffing" never happened, but was merely mocked up in a parking lot."

 ## Sticking points

M A "conspiracy theory" is an alternative account of a particular event, often conflicting with the generally accepted version.

U "Public opinion polls" are surveys designed to gauge attitudes on a particular matter.

D Explain what you think is meant by a "convention." (In this instance, a convention is a gathering of individuals who meet at an agreed time and place to discuss a shared interest.)

 ## Thinkantation

Fake some photographic evidence to support a fictional event.

 ## Editors' note

Conspiracy theorists never translate to conspiracy activists; in other words, they are full of hot air. Not unlike wolves ...

PIGGY PROMPTS

Name the CEO of Underhammed Marketing.

Sales of bricks at the local hardware stores rocketed. They'd recently employed the services of Underhammed Marketing.

Last year's annual convention of Huffing Deniers was canceled due to poor attendance. No one believed it was actually taking place.

Which local sports team does Underhammed Marketing sponsor?

37. THE PURSUIT OF PORK

Your Title: ....

Ponder

What drove the wolf to try to commit such atrocities?

Nudges

- Do you think the wolf was starving? Was he hunting out of necessity?

  e.g., "No, if the wolf was genuinely starving, he wouldn't play with his food."

- Did the wolf take pleasure in the thrill of the chase?

  e.g., "Wolfie has a certain theatrical bent. He enjoyed creating a narrative that showcased his prowess."

- Did the wolf perceive himself to be a villain?

  e.g., "The wolf perceived himself to be a lovable rogue—with psychotic tendencies."

PIGGY PROMPTS

If you're a food lover, can feeling hungry
be described as a crime of passion?

Wolfie claimed he wanted to
digest the report in full.

Professor Quack was a renowned expert
in his field. Unfortunately, he wasn't
in his field when counseling Wolfie.

Would you say the wolf had
an eating disorder?

Sticking points

M "Psychiatrists" are doctors who specialize in the treatment of mental health and well-being.

U Someone possessing a "theatrical bent" has a tendency to use exaggerated language and mannerisms, as if performing on the stage.

D How would you describe a "lovable rogue"? (Someone who breaks the law, but has sufficient charm to remain popular in the eyes of others.)

 ## Thinkantation

Design and make a comfortable couch to recline upon. Remember to open up ...

 ## Editors' note

The wolf has a history of psychiatric disorders. He ate the psychiatrist.

38. ASSAULT AND PEPPER

Your Title: ....

Ponder

How did the pigs manage to prepare a large pot of boiling water amid the chaos?

Nudges

- A watched kettle never boils, let alone a large cooking pot. How did the pigs find the time when faced with the impending assault?

  e.g., "They added a large amount of seasoning— salt water boils more quickly."

- Where did the pigs manage to source that amount of water from? They must have needed gallons.

  e.g., "Big Pig is an avid historian: After studying the ancient Romans, he ensured he built his house adjacent to a stream. His first task was to construct a simple irrigation system, allowing him to access water on tap."[4]

- Why did Wolfie not "feel the heat" a little sooner and amend his plan of attack?

  e.g., "A wolf's fur is extra thick around its hindquarters to insulate from extreme cold. The

---

4 Hence known as the "stream of consciousness."

wolf was not able to register the temperature differential until it was too late."

Sticking points

M An "irrigation system" is designed to supply plants with water at regular intervals.

U "Insulation" maintains the temperature of someone or something by wrapping them/it in a suitable material, thus maintaining the core temperature for longer.

D How much is a gallon? (The UK [imperial] gallon—different from the American gallon—is 4.54609 liters. Alternatively, 1 American gallon = 8 pints.)

Thinkantation

Design a drainage system for transferring a gallon of water from one place to another.

Editors' note

Apparently, wolf is best served with added thyme.

PIGGY PROMPTS

How did Big Pig acquire his knowledge of physics?

Do the pigs know how to use a microwave?

Or maybe the wolf is extra thick?

39. FASTER FOOD

Your Title: ....

Ponder

It would have been a lot easier for the wolf if he'd opted for a burger and fries instead. Why didn't he just order takeout?

Nudges

❧ The wolf must have been very hungry—and got even hungrier with all that huffing and puffing. Why not grab a kebab?

e.g., "Kosta's Kebabs serve a wide variety of dishes, of which 'edible' is not one."

❧ All that running around was bound to cause indigestion. Surely there was a more civilized eating plan?

e.g., "Wolfie's plan was to simultaneously burn and consume calories, resulting in zero weight gain."[5]

❧ It's been noted that Wolfie had failed his driving test. Do you think not being able to use the drive-through somehow fueled his ire?

e.g., "Yes, Wolfie stated he was going to get a 'shake' one way or another."

---

5   Also known as "bon-bon neutral."

PIGGY PROMPTS

Wind was most definitely a problem (for the pigs).

What's on Kosta's menu?

How do you make a pig shake?

Sticking points

M A "kebab" usually consists of a combination of meat, fish or vegetables, sometimes roasted or grilled on a skewer.

U "Calories" can be used to measure the amount of energy in food.

D What is meant by "heartburn"? (The unpleasant burning feeling when acid from the stomach rises up into the food pipe.)

 Thinkantation

Design a label for the wolf's heartburn remedy. Don't forget to list the ingredients.

 Editors' note

Heartburn proved to be the least of the wolf's problems—after dropping into the boiling pot.

40. CLEANING FLUID?

Your Title: ....

 Ponder

The whole episode left a trail of destruction. Was there a successful clean-up operation?

 Nudges

- Most of the damage had been cleared away by the following day. Was there some sort of cover-up?

  e.g., "Porktown had won the title of Best Kept Village for the previous two years. Mayoral candidate Councillor Fang Django had pinned his hopes on a third."

- The clean-up operation was headed by Mucky Business, coincidentally founded by the three little pigs' uncle. Is there more to this than just a coincidence?

  e.g., "Shares in Mucky Business spiked as a result of the extra work. Maybe the wolf wasn't the only one trying to make a killing."

> There is a suggestion that Fang and Wolfie are related. Could events have been contrived for purely political gain?

e.g., "Without serious crime, no one can promise to be tough on crime. Django received public support for his zero-tolerance stance."

 ## Sticking points

M "Shares" are the equal parts into which a company's worth is divided, entitling the holder to a proportion of the profits.

U "Political gain" refers to acquiring support and/ or advantage for the views and opinions of a particular political party.

D How would you describe a "zero-tolerance stance"? (A no-compromise approach to anyone who contravenes accepted behaviors and expectations.)

 ## Thinkantation

Itemize the amount of weekly recycling for an average resident of Porktown.

 ## Editors' note

Politics can be a dirty business. Literally.

PIGGY PROMPTS

Mucky Business is diversifying into what?

Apparently, "where there's swine, there's grime."

Can wolves be green?

How would you describe Django's brand of politics?

41. BRED MAKER

Your Title: ....

Ponder

Little is known about the wolf. Who is this mysterious predator?

Nudges

❧ Where has Wolfie come from?

> e.g., "The wolf arrived seemingly out of nowhere and vanished into thin air—an ephemeral harbinger."[6]

❧ What would bring a wolf to a quiet law-abiding place such as Porktown?

> e.g., "I think the wolf was intent on making a name for himself."

❧ Why did the wolf threaten all that huffing and puffing?

> e.g., "It sounded cooler than warning of intermittent inhalation and exhalation."

---

6 Or a wolf without a tale.

PIGGY PROMPTS

What would be a more appropriate name for Wolfie?

Can you find Wolfie?

Sticking points

M "Predators" are wild animals who hunt or prey on other animals.

U An "ephemeral harbinger" is someone or something who fleetingly appears to signal forthcoming events.

D What is meant by "making a name for himself"? (Endeavoring to become famous or well-known.)

Thinkantation

Create a magnification device. Use it to make a mountain out of a molehill.

Editors' note

Sorry, Wolfie's hiding. But maybe you can figure out his hiding place?

42. HUFFING-TOWN POST

Your Title: ....

Ponder

After making a hasty departure, the wolf was never seen again. Why didn't he return to settle some scores?

Nudges

➤ Following his humiliating fall from grace, surely Wolfie needed to salvage some respect?

e.g., "While he would have loved to get his paws on the pork, the wolf was more concerned with saving his burnt behind than saving face."

➤ Where did the wolf go to recuperate and lick his wounds?

e.g., "There are unconfirmed reports of him spending a stint in rehab, attempting to curb his piggy addiction."

➤ Did the wolf lie low for a while? When was he next seen again?

e.g., "Following treatment, Wolfie found a temporary job as a debt collector. Unfortunately, the general public was still intent on keeping the wolf from the door and his contract was soon terminated."

Sticking points

M To "settle scores" is to get even and avenge a grievance or an injury.

U "Rehabilitation" is the process of recovering from a particular incident, illness or injury.

D What is meant by an "unconfirmed report"? (A report or rumor with no definite proof as to whether it is true or not.)

 # Thinkantation

Create an alternative identity for the wolf, enabling him to start a new life elsewhere.

 # Editors' note

Wolves never look back; they prefer something new to get their teeth into.

PIGGY PROMPTS

Who's the source of the
"unconfirmed reports"?

What's the name of the rehab clinic?

Is a rehabilitated wolf more
or less dangerous?

43. PIG E DAY

Your Title: ....

Ponder

What did the three little pigs do to commemorate the momentous events of that day, lest they forget?

Nudges

❥ Do you think the anniversary is a happy or sad occasion?

e.g., "The occasion is quite poignant, as the community considers the true price of bacon."

❥ What's the format of the day?

e.g., "After a minute's silence, the community distributes food to local wolves in a show of reconciliation. Girls in red hoods are discouraged from partaking."

❥ How do the wolves view the annual show of remembrance?

e.g., "While some deny the 'huffing' took place, others lay a wreath in a show of solidarity. A few quietly suggest that the wolf was the real victim."

PIGGY PROMPTS

The How's Down organization aims to educate pigs with amnesia about the perils of home-making.

What do the community members wear to show their support?

It's been argued that the wolf's only crime was to be full of hot air—of which many of us are guilty.

The opposition group, Howling, aims to provide a voice for repressed wolves.

Sticking points

M A "poignant" occasion is one that is touching or moving, and often tinged with sadness.

U An act of "remembrance" involves thinking about those who died for the good of others—usually in the service of their country.

D What is meant by "commercialization"? (The process of developing an idea or product to the point where it can be marketed and sold.)

 Thinkantation

Construct a fitting memorial in remembrance of the "huffing."

 Editors' note

There have been complaints about the increasing commercialization of events—commemorative hot-air balloon races and novelty wolf whistles have been branded as poor taste.

44. A PIG DIFFERENCE

Your Title: ....

Ponder

In a land not so far away, every year the wolf community celebrates the brave escape of Wolfie from three marauding pigs. Has the wolf become a folk hero?

Nudges

❧ Why would the wolves attempt to distort history?

e.g., "No one likes to be associated with a loser. With the haze of hindsight and a little social compliance, it's easy to reframe 'loser' as 'victim.'"

❧ Surely it's obvious that the wolf was the aggressor?

e.g., "It was the pigs who drew first blood. A little huffing and puffing is not a crime, after all."

❧ Does the wolf ever speak about his exploits?

e.g., "Wolfie has become something of a recluse. He's hiding from the truth."

Sticking points

M "Hindsight" refers to the understanding of an event that comes only after it has taken place.

U A "recluse" is someone who tends to live a solitary life and avoid other people.

D How would you describe a "parallel universe"? (An imaginary universe that mirrors our own, where events usually take a different course.)

 Thinkantation

Construct a parallel universe that the wolf can inhabit.

 Editors' note

Contrary to perceived wisdom, it can be possible for two opposing viewpoints to be right. Just as both can be wrong, so the converse must also be true (or false).

PIGGY PROMPTS

Many wolves and pigs demonstrate the capacity to suspend disbelief—even adults remain hopeful that the tooth fairy might visit (otherwise known as the tooth fairly).

What other fictional characters do the animals believe in?

Contrary to popular opinion, wolves are not illiterate. Some like nothing more than to devour a good book (particularly when it's being read by a pig).

Do you need a fairy to make a fairy tale?

45. AEROPIG CAPACITY

Your Title: ....

Ponder

While fleeing the wolf, Little Pig and Middle Pig demonstrated impressive acceleration. How were they able to outrun the wolf?

Nudges

➤ Do you think the pigs were fast, or was the wolf simply dragging his paws?

  e.g., "The pigs had explosive acceleration, developed over months of core strength training in the gym."

➤ Surely the wolf should have had little trouble keeping up?

  e.g., "He could have run like the wind, but thought he'd better conserve his energy."

➤ But really, how did they manage to get away?

  e.g., "Even the pigs don't seem to know—their memories seem muddy."

PIGGY PROMPTS

Can a pig be a gym rat?

What's the name of the pigs' gym?

Can a rat be a gym pig?

The most commonly reported sports-related injury for pigs is a pulled hamstring (also known as pulled pork).

Sticking points

M "Aerobic capacity" refers to the body's ability to consume oxygen, and is used as an indication of someone's physical fitness.

U Your "hamstring" refers to the area of muscle at the back of the upper leg (above knee height).

D What is "backgammon"? (A two-player board game that involves rolling dice in an attempt to remove counters.)

 ## Thinkantation

Design a suitable outfit for one of the pigs to work out in.

 ## Editors' note

Most pigs prefer more sedentary sports—darts, billiards and the like. Backgammon can also be a popular pastime.

46. SERENDIPIGGY

Your Title: ....

Ponder

By a fortunate series of coincidences, it seems some good has come from the whole affair. Can you elaborate?

Nudges

➤ What effect did the lucky escape have on the pigs?

e.g., "One of the pigs found Hog,[7] another built a highly profitable construction company and the third makes a lucrative living as a much-in-demand after-dinner speaker."

➤ What became of the wolf?

e.g., "There are conflicting reports about the whereabouts of the wolf, but he is reputedly in negotiations to turn his life story into a film."[8]

➤ What effect did the events have on Mr. and Mrs. Pig?

e.g., "No lasting damage. Mrs. Pig has recently released her first book: a parenting guide entitled *Tough Mudder: Being Cruel to be Kind*."

---

7   Where did he find him?

8   *Gone with the Wind* has been mooted as a possible title.

Sticking points

M   People who are "superstitious" believe the occurrence of certain events or actions may cause other (completely unrelated) events to take place.

U   An "after-dinner speaker" is someone who is paid to make an entertaining or motivational speech at a formal dinner gathering.

D   What is meant by "negotiations"? (The process where people agree on an outcome by discussion and compromise.)

 ## Thinkantation

Design and make a lucky charm to bring the pigs further good fortune.

 ## Editors' note

If life is like a box of chocolates, then the pigs have found the truffles.

PIGGY PROMPTS

Animals are not generally superstitious. Apart from rabbits, who need to stay on their toes ...

47. WOOD YOU BELIEVE IT?

Your Title: ....

Ponder

When the wolf approached the house made of brick, his huffing and puffing made no impact. Why did the wooden door remain intact when the house made of sticks had previously been obliterated?

Nudges

◗ Why did the wooden door resist the wolf's advances?

e.g., "The door had been treated with a special puff-proof anti-wolf retardant, ensuring the wolf's huffing was to no avail."

◗ The wolf had already exerted himself by the time he reached the house of the Big Pig. Was he out of breath?

e.g., "Yes, the wolf had already undertaken a considerable workout and was not able to generate the same force."

◗ So why did the wooden window frames remain intact?

e.g., "They were triple paned, enabling them to weather the eye of the storm."

PIGGY PROMPTS

What's the name of the anti-wolf retardant?

Is the eye of the storm similar to the eye of the tiger?

Can a tiger have the eye of a wolf?

Why did the retardant work on the wolf—he wasn't an auntie?

Sticking points

M To "obliterate" something means to completely destroy it.

U A "retardant" is a protective layer that can be painted or sprayed onto a particular object.

D What does the term "the eye of the storm" mean? (A period of relative calm following a time of unrest.)

 ## Thinkantation

Construct a portable door mechanism allowing you to access new places at will.

 ## Editors' note

Apparently, when one door closes another one opens. It has something to do with a pressure differential.

48. CARELESS WHISPORK

Your Title: ....

Ponder

When the pigs returned to the family home after their ordeal, what sort of reception did they receive from their parents?

Nudges

❥ Were Mr. and Mrs. Pig relieved to see their offspring home safe?

e.g., "Neither parent was impressed to see the children back so soon, especially as they had not managed to change the locks yet."

❥ Did Mr. and Mrs. Pig believe their children were in some way culpable for the unwanted attentions of the wolf?

e.g., "It was no secret that Big Pig was regularly bad-mouthing the wolf in the local bars and clubs. It seems the wolf was intent on setting the record straight."[9]

---

9 List some of the records the wolf had in his collection.

> What happened in the days following the siblings' inglorious return home?

> e.g., "Little Pig tried to continue her paper route, only to find it had been taken by another girl in a red hood."[10]

 Sticking points

M "Bad-mouthing" is to say unkind things about someone, usually without their knowledge.

U Something described as "inglorious" might suggest that it was embarrassing or regrettable.

D What is meant by "setting the record straight"? (Explaining the truth regarding a particular event or situation, therefore countering a hitherto inaccurate representation.)

 Thinkantation

Invent a "lucky escape" for someone who narrowly avoids getting into hot water.

 Editors' note

The front page headline of *The Porky Post* exclaimed "SWINE PHEW!"

---

10 What was the clue for 3 down in the crossword puzzle of today's issue of *The Porky Post*?

PIGGY PROMPTS

Apparently Big Pig accused Wolfie of dressing like a grandma.

What were the local newspaper headlines the following day?

49. STY, STY AGAIN

Your Title: ....

Ponder

After the trauma of leaving home the first time, how long was it before the pigs were able to venture forth a second time?

Nudges

❥ Did the pigs require therapy?

> e.g., "Little Pig required a course of HBT (Hognative Behavioral Therapy) before feeling ready to face the world again."

❥ Did they take steps to minimize the risk of wolf interference?

> e.g., "Yes, very small steps—staying out of sight where possible."

❥ Did the pigs learn a lesson? Is there a moral to this story?

> e.g., "Yes—always cry wolf!"

PIGGY PROMPTS

Did the wolf require therapy of some sort?
Or maybe therapy for being out of sorts?

How do the residents of Porktown
view the wind of change?

Middle Pig found yoga (or "hoga") beneficial
to his recuperation.

Sticking points

M A "moral" is a message or a lesson that can be learned through the telling of a story.

U Being "out of sorts" suggests feeling slightly unwell or unhappy.

D How would you describe a "wind of change"? (A marked shift in the presiding attitude and opinions of more than one person.)

 ## Thinkantation

Design a plaque to commemorate the pigs' narrow escape.

 ## Editors' note

The wolf has made a partial recovery—he's blowing hot and cold.

50. PORK JOBS?

Your Title: ....

Ponder

Do the cast of "The Three Little Pigs" wish they had made different career choices?

Nudges

❧ Perhaps the pigs should have ventured further afield to seek their fortune?

e.g., "Middle Pig had considered joining the navy to travel the world, but thought he might get sea sick.

❧ Why did all three pigs stay so close to home?

e.g., "None of the pigs had ventured far from home before—they preferred an in-law unit."

❧ Why do the pigs seem incapable of thinking for themselves?

e.g., "They're naturally cautious; none of them were keen on trot-footing it out of town."

PIGGY PROMPTS

Flying pigs? Maybe the air force would
have been more appropriate.

Little Pig didn't want to be
seen as a chops-worth.

Middle Pig did consider an apprenticeship,
but again, he thought it meant going to sea.

Sticking points

M A "beret" is a soft, round, flat hat—usually associated with the people of France.

U An "apprenticeship" is a job that also provides training, enabling you to acquire the skills required to become proficient.

D How would you describe an "in-law unit"? (A building that is built on the same property as an existing dwelling.)

 Thinkantation

Design and make a beret for a member of the Swine Sea Corps (SSC).

 Editors' note

Pigs are not renowned for making astute career choices. They tend to make a pig's ear of things.

51. UN-MEN-TIONABLE?

Your Title: ....

Ponder

Throughout the tale there is a notable absence of humans. Whatever happened to mankind?

Nudges

- Have *Homo sapiens* become extinct, or merely taken an alternative evolutionary path?

  e.g., "Humans have increasingly occupied a virtual reality, to the extent that they now exist solely online."

- Is humanity evident in the behavior of the different animals?

  e.g., "Family love ultimately prevailed, although the siblings made something of a sow's ear of it."

- What is the future of Planet Earth?

  e.g., "The unstoppable and inexorable rise of pigkind (the Pig Power Movement)."[11]

---

11 Also known as the Think Pig campaign.

PIGGY PROMPTS

Download the Being app for a
dose of virtual humanity.

The rival Blown Out campaign argues
for greater wolf integration.

A pig's constitution could best
be described as robust.

Sticking points

M *"Homo sapiens"* is the scientific name for the species of primate to which human beings belong.

U The word "constitution" can be used to describe physical and emotional characteristics, as well as the rules agreed upon for running an organization.

D Can you explain what is meant by "inexorable"? (Something that is inevitable and unstoppable.)

 ## Thinkantation

Design an unmovable object to be met by an unstoppable force.

 ## Editors' note

Pig movements can be a messy business.

52. CULTURAL COOPERATION

Your Title: ....

Ponder

Linguistic and cultural influences mean that translated versions may differ. How does the story of "The Three Little Pigs" vary around the world?

Nudges

❥ Japanese pigs don't "oink"—they "boo-boo." Does this change things?

e.g., "A samurai pig may have reacted slightly differently to the advances of the wolf ..."

❥ Have cultural differences altered the outcome of the "Three Little Pigs" story in different countries?

e.g., "There are subtle differences between East and West: Eastern nations include a meditative element. The wolf doesn't just huff but performs several sun salutations too."

❥ In some countries a pack of wolves is pursued by a ravenous (and windy) pig. How did the marauding pig threaten the fleeing wolves?

e.g., "He threatened harassment and intimidation and strongly recommended self-preservation."

Sticking points

M "Samurais" were revered Japanese medieval warriors.

U "Salutations" describe a series of movements performed when practicing yoga.

D What is meant by "cultural differences"? (Variations in the way of life, beliefs, laws and traditions associated with different countries.)

 Thinkantation

Craft the award for the Best Foreign Film dramatization of *Pig 3*.

 Editors' note

Wolves often speak the mantra "peace and love" when referring to their pork counterparts. Which particular piece varies from wolf to wolf.

PIGGY PROMPTS

Does murdering a curry make you guilty? Does it depend on the flavor?

Which country is the pig murder capital of the world?

Name a popular "hoga" position.

The pigs' tale varies from nation to nation. Some are more curly than others.

53. BASKET CASE

Your Title: ....

Ponder

Why did Little Red Riding Hood's mother send her on an errand in the first place? Surely it was much too risky?

Nudges

❧ Did Mrs. Riding Hood fully appreciate the potential for disaster?

e.g., "Mrs. Hood believed in 'tough love.' And Granny Hood was demanding—and even tougher."

❧ Did Little Red Riding Hood experience any trepidation on venturing into the deep, dark forest with her basket of treats?

e.g., "She took the view that there's nothing to fear except fear itself. That was until she bumped into a wolf impersonating her grandma."

❧ What's Little Red Riding Hood got to do with "The Three Little Pigs" anyway?!

e.g., "Ms. Riding Hood is widely acknowledged as one of the world's leading experts and foremost authorities on wolf attacks and rehabilitation."

PIGGY PROMPTS

Did Little Red Riding Hood have any specific difficulties preventing her from recognizing that a wolf was dressed up in her granny's nightie?

Why was Little Red Riding Hood walking rather than riding?

What's with the whole, "All the better to ..." routine? Why didn't the wolf just get on with it?

Little Red Riding Hood was so called because she liked to ride her luck.

Sticking points

M An "errand" is usually a short trip to deliver or collect something.

U "Trepidation" describes a feeling of fear or anxiety about something that may happen.

D What do you think is meant by the phrase "there is nothing to fear except fear itself"? (The worry is often worse than actually experiencing the event causing it.)

 # Thinkantation

Make one of grandma's cakes that looks good enough to eat (but is actually inedible).

 # Editors' note

Questions are being asked regarding why a wolf with "priors" was allowed out, only to reoffend.

54. BOAR-ED STUPID

Your Title: ....

Ponder

Of all the traditional tales, is the cast of "The Three Little Pigs" by far the dumbest?

Nudges

❥ Why did the pigs leave home before they had even started building their new abodes?

e.g., "Pigs evidently can't think ahead. They can't even think 'abehind.'"

❥ Surely they must compare favorably with Goldilocks?

e.g., "Fair point—she failed to bear in mind the consequences of her actions."

❥ Why hadn't the wolf learned his lesson?

e.g., "Good point—with his track record, you'd think the wolf would be building bridges rather than blowing down houses."

PIGGY PROMPTS

If a leopard can't change its spots,
can a wolf do any better?

Why is the pig wearing suspenders?

The bare-faced cheeks were
reputedly quite sizable.

Is the wolf fur real?

Sticking points

M An "abode" is another name for a house or home.

U "Bare-faced cheek" describes someone who does something clearly wrong or inappropriate but displays no shame or remorse.

D What is meant by "the thin end of the wedge"? (The beginning of a potentially harmful development.)

 ## Thinkantation

Create and make a wedge with a suitably thick end.

 ## Editors' note

The cast of "The Emperor's New Clothes" was actually awarded the "Dumbo" in recognition of their naked ambition (and a little bare-faced cheek).

55. BIG BAD-MOUTHING

Your Title: ....

Ponder

For years pigs have had to endure prejudice, negative stereotyping and repression. Is any of it warranted?

Nudges

❥ Did the pigs really think they could put up a house from just a few bits of twig and straw?

e.g., "They really had no idea about materials being fit for purpose. In fact, pigs have no comprehension of the word 'fit.'"

❥ Perhaps the pigs deserved everything they got. Were they nasty pieces of work?

e.g., "The pigs were selfless do-gooders, and would do anything to help themselves."

❥ The wolf has long campaigned to clear his name. Why has his fight proved hitherto unsuccessful?

e.g., "Because of a reputation for literally blowing away the opposition."

PIGGY PROMPTS

Perhaps the wolf was the real victim—he's the one who ended up in hot water.

Shoddy workmanship suggests the pigs evidently cut a lot more than just corners.

The pigs weren't happy; they'd got "beef." Or possibly not.

Sticking points

M Being "prejudiced" means to form an opinion without knowing the relevant facts surrounding a particular situation.

U A "do-gooder" is someone who is generally well-meaning but whose interference can cause more harm than good.

D What is meant by "muckraking"? (Publicly exposing the misconduct of prominent figures.)

 Thinkantation

Make note of an action you can take to make a difference. Plan on a time and place to take that action.

 Editors' note

To be fair, pigs don't generally have a good word to say about anyone; they have a propensity for muckraking.

56. SOW FAR, SOW GOOD

Your Title: ....

Ponder

"The Three Little Pigs" is supposed to be a timeless classic—an enduring tale that captivates successive generations. What's the appeal?

Nudges

- Three siblings decide to set up home and make a rush job of it. So what?

  e.g., "It's an emotional rollercoaster—a very moving story."[12]

- Can a pig really fulfill a heroic role?

  e.g., "Pigs can be heroes, if only for just one day."

- Three slackers narrowly avoid the attention of a psychopathic wolf. Does the story bear any relevance to modern day society?

  e.g., "Not really. Goldilocks would probably draw greater parallels."

---

12 What other rides are there in an emotional theme park?

Sticking points

M An "intuitive" person acts according to what they feel to be the right course of action without careful consideration of the facts.

U An "emotional rollercoaster" describes experiencing very different emotions associated with a particular situation.

D How would you define a "slacker"? (Someone who actively avoids doing their fair share of work.)

 Thinkantation

Construct a heroic pork roll.

 Editors' note

Pigs can be very intuitive: One that shows great foresight can be described as a "pig seer."

PIGGY PROMPTS

There are reported sightings of the infamous pig superhero, the Almighty Boar.

Draw a selection of Goldilocks' parallels.

PIGS is a four-letter word. What other four-letter words can you think of to describe them?

57. SAFE STY?

Your Title: ....

Ponder

When the pigs eventually rebuilt, what concessions did they make to the possibility of a puff attack?

Nudges

❥ Which building material did they choose?

e.g., "While brick was the obvious choice, the pigs eventually opted for plastic doors and windows over wooden ones (splintering opinion)."

❥ Did they install security systems?

e.g., "A state-of-the-art vacuum generator was installed to nullify any potential huffing and puffing."

❥ What would the pigs do in the event of a further attack?

e.g., "They routinely practice various escape drills, and rehearse anti-wolf protocol. All three pigs have attended assertiveness classes."

PIGGY PROMPTS

The pigs installed a secret getaway tunnel. Where did it lead from and to?

This fondness for plastic extends to cosmetic surgery. What is the most popular procedure for pigs?

What is the name of the world-renowned animal cosmetic surgeon?

The pigs declined the option of a new identity—The Three Little (...) didn't quite work.

Sticking points

M A "concession" refers to something that is allowed or tolerated in order to satisfy a need imposed by others.

U A "vacuum" is an empty space where there is no air or any other gas. Vacuum cleaners use a vacuum to suck up dirt from the floor.

D How would you describe a "siege"? (A siege is typically where enemy forces surround a particular place, cutting off essential supplies with the aim of forcing a surrender.)

 ## Thinkantation

Construct a drilling mechanism that would enable the three pigs to escape if their house was under siege.

 ## Editors' note

Wolves are not renowned for dealing with rejection (or having the wind taken out of their sails).

58. BIG BAD LANGUAGE

Your Title: ....

Ponder

If you're a pig, to be referred to as a "fat pig" is praise indeed. Which characters in the story are most deserving of insults and abuse?

Nudges

- Mr. and Mrs. Pig are a disgrace. Surely, expelling their ill-prepared offspring from the family home equates to gross negligence?

  e.g., "They have subsequently become the victims of a targeted online hate campaign, regularly being trolled on social media. The troll who lives beneath the trip-trap bridge has been interviewed in connection with the alleged offenses."

- Are all the pigs victims here? The wolf is solely responsible for unwarranted physical and emotional pain and suffering.

  e.g., "Wolves have no conscience. While you may hear someone cry wolf, you won't hear a wolf cry."

- Perhaps the wolf and the pigs should move on, kiss and make up?

  e.g., "Neither animal is keen on kissing, and only Mrs. Pig and Middle Pig feel comfortable wearing make-up."

 ## Sticking points

M Your "conscience" describes an inner voice, suggesting the correct course of action (or inaction) in a particular situation.

U "Profanities" are examples of unkind, offensive and insulting language.

D What is meant by "trolling"? (Deliberately and repeatedly causing offense on social media forums.)

 ## Thinkantation

Compile an original list of profanities and expletives that the various characters can hurl at one another.

 ## Editors' note

Those easily offended by bad language should not have read this far.

PIGGY PROMPTS

Criminal fences are not to be confused with garden fences, who are typically fine, upstanding members of the community.

What does a fence have to do with trolling?

Fences are not adverse to trolling; it complements their criminal résumé. (Similar to the garden rake, who will always call a spade a spade.)

59. GROWTH MUDSET

Your Title: ....

Ponder

Why would anyone want to write a growth mindset book about "The Three Little Pigs" anyway?

Nudges

➤ What do pigs know about a growth mindset?

e.g., "Absolutely nothing, except perhaps for Big Pig, who didn't opt for a quick fix."

➤ Can you really "grow" your mind?[13]

e.g., "The wolf had a good go at blowing his mind, so maybe anything is possible."

➤ Is this book likely to be made into a film?

e.g., "Unlikely—they'd never allow pigs onto a red carpet."

---

13 Apparently the secret is to sty, sty and sty again.

PIGGY PROMPTS

Professor Wolfie (BAd) lectures on the importance of getting your teeth into something.

What does "BAd" stand for?

Pigs extol the virtues of operating in threes (a safety sty-angle).

Sticking points

M A "growth mindset" is the belief that ability can be improved through dedication and hard work.

U "Red carpets" are typically rolled out for special occasions and line the route that important people are going to walk along.

D Can you explain what is meant by a "virtue"? (A trait or quality that is deemed to be morally good.)

 Thinkantation

Create a replica of a pig's brain (or a thinking cap).

 Editors' note

Pigs are ideal for illustrating the importance of a growth mindset. They have a wealth of experience in extricating themselves from being stuck in the mud.

60. PULLED PORK

Your Title: ....

Ponder

So this is the end or, more specifically, a bookend. What was the point?

Nudges

- Is there a moral to this story? Will humanity benefit from the true story of "The Three Little Pigs"?

  e.g., "The tale works on several levels: The pigs are clueless, their parents are heartless, the wolf is shameless and the possibilities are boundless."

- Pigs and wolves. Wolves and pigs. Can you think of an alternative combination?

  e.g., "Three little elephants pursued by a goldfish might make waves."[14]

- What's next?

  e.g., "The pigs are launching a range of merchandise, and have already released a pop single."

---

14 Something to pond-er over.

PIGGY PROMPTS

The tail, however, is another matter entirely.

What's the name of the pop single?

The wolf, by comparison, has already blown it.

Sticking points

M Being "clueless" suggests a complete lack of knowledge or competence in a particular field.

U "Merchandise" is another word for goods that are bought and sold.

D How would you describe "making waves"? (Challenging accepted thinking or practices in a way that might leave an impression.)

 Thinkantation

Design an item for the new range of merchandise.

 Editors' note

Editors don't always know best. Sometimes they choose to make no comment.

ACKNOWLEDGMENTS

We'd like to acknowledge our indebtedness to all those teachers who so magnificently refuse to sacrifice their delight in language to the demands of curricular diktat, and who manage to keep their students critically engaged, curious and creative as a result. You know what we know: that students who embrace challenges, who have to think critically and creatively, and who develop a deep learning stamina in the process are the students who end up doing really well—in performance terms anyway. But for you (and for them), exceptional performance creeps up as a secondary gift to an explicit focus on the love of learning and an intrinsic interest in challenging tasks for their own sake. We suspect you'll forgive the tone and aspirations of this book, which is based on a profound respect for students' capacity to rise beyond stage and developmental expectations, because you know that Joseph Renzulli was correct in observing that "A rising tide lifts all ships." Thank you for raising the tide ...